Our American Family™

I Am
Vietnamese
American

Felice Blanc

The Rosen Publishing Group's
PowerKids Press™
New York

Published in 1997 by The Rosen Publishing Group, Inc.
29 East 21st Street, New York, NY 10010

First Edition

Book Design: Erin McKenna

Photo Credits: Cover © George Ancone/International Stock Photo; background © Icon Comm/FPG International Corp.; p. 4 © Scott Barrow/International Stock Photo; p. 7 © Jean Kugler/FPG International Corp.; p. 8 © FPG International Corp.; p. 11 © Alvars Loginovs/FPG International Corp.; p. 12 © Henry R. Wilms/FPG International Corp.; p. 15 © R. Richardson/H. Armstrong Roberts Inc.; p. 16 © Dennie Cody/FPG International Corp.; p. 19 © Joe Smoljan/International Stock Photo; p. 20 © K. Rice/H. Armstrong Roberts Inc.

Blanc, Felice.
   I Am Vietnamese American / by Felice Blanc.
       p.   cm. — (Our American Family)
   Includes index.
   Summary: A Vietnamese American discusses his traditions, heritage, culture, and pride in his family.
   ISBN 0-8239-5009-3
   1. Vietnamese Americans—Juvenile literature. [1. Vietnamese Americans—Juvenile literature.]
   I. Title. II. Series.
E184.V53S78 1997
973'.04592—dc21
                                                        97-3582
                                                         CIP

Manufactured in the United States of America   AC

Contents

Tran

Hi! My name is Tran. In Vietnam, where my parents were born, people usually put their family name first and their first name last. Our family name is Nguyen, so my full name is Nguyen Tran. I live with my parents and my grandmother in New Orleans, Louisiana. My grandmother, mother, and father came to America from Hanoi. Hanoi is a big city that is also the capital of Vietnam.

◀ Members of your family may have interesting things to tell you about your history.

Vietnam

Vietnam is a narrow country in Southeast Asia, south of China. It's bordered by the South China Sea on one side and three countries—Laos, Cambodia, and China—on the other. Three huge rivers run through Vietnam—the Saigon River, the Mekong River, and the Red River. Some Vietnamese people live near the ocean and fish for a living. Many others work on small rice farms called **paddies** (PAD-eez). And some people work in the cities. My parents worked as teachers in Hanoi. Both the people and the language of Vietnam are called Vietnamese.

Most of the land in Vietnam is green and fertile. ▶

Ho Chi Minh

In the late 1800s, the French gained control of Vietnam. The French didn't treat the Vietnamese well, and a man named Ho Chi Minh wanted **independence** (in-dee-PEN-dents) for his people. He promised the Vietnamese that they would be free from French rule. This finally happened in 1954, when Vietnam defeated the French. Vietnam was then split into two countries and Ho Chi Minh became president of North Vietnam. But when he died in 1969, Vietnam was in the middle of a different war. This is when my parents began to think about coming to the U.S.

◀ Ho Chi Minh spent most of his life working for Vietnam's freedom from France.

9

The Vietnam War

The Vietnam War started in 1954 when North Vietnam and South Vietnam began fighting against each other. The United States got involved in this war and tried to help the South Vietnamese set up a **democracy** (dem-AH-kra-see). Thousands of people, including Americans and North and South Vietnamese, died or were badly hurt. The war ended in 1975 and Vietnam was **reunited** (ree-yoo-NY-ted) in 1976. However, times were still very hard for most Vietnamese. Many of my aunts and uncles were involved in this war.

Over 500,000 men and women were sent from the United States to help South Vietnam. ▶

Refugees

Most people who move to America from another country save their money and plan their trip for a long time. However, some people are **refugees** (REF-yoo-jeez). Refugees leave their country in a hurry because their lives are in danger. They usually have to give up all their belongings. Sometimes they even have to leave without their families. Right after the Vietnam War, my parents and grandmother came to America as refugees.

◄ Many Vietnamese left their country as refugees, hoping for a better life in the United States.

13

Vietnamese

When my parents came to America, they didn't speak any English. They only spoke Vietnamese. Vietnamese used to be written with **characters** (KAYR-ak-terz) instead of letters, like Chinese and Japanese. But unlike other Asian languages, Vietnamese has changed. Today, it's written with the same letters as English. Vietnamese is a **tonal** (TOH-nul) language. That means that the same word can mean different things if you change the tone used to say the word.

Vietnamese is a blend of many languages, ▶ including Chinese and French.

Buddhism

Like many other Vietnamese, my family practices a religion called **Buddhism** (BOOD-izm). Buddhism was started about 2,500 years ago by a man named Gautama. He spent a long time thinking about the best way to live, and then traveled throughout Asia in order to teach people his beliefs. He believed that people don't need to own lots of things to be happy. He was called the Buddha, which means the **enlightened** (en-LYT-end), or wise, one.

◀ Buddhists often build altars to worship the Buddha. This altar is in a cave in Vietnam.

Tet

At the end of January or the beginning of February, Vietnamese people have a huge New Year's celebration called Tet. Right before this holiday, my father carves pictures into small blocks of wood for all the kids in my family. Then we dip the blocks into paint and press them onto colored paper to make prints. Tet is the most important Vietnamese holiday of the year. We decorate the house with lots of flowers, eat special foods, and give our parents the block prints as presents. They give us presents too.

Tet is a time to celebrate with family. ▶

Food

My grandmother loves to cook Vietnamese food. Many dishes have cabbage, a vegetable which is like lettuce, in them. Almost every meal includes rice. Sometimes my grandmother makes rice pancakes that she fills with vegetables. Other times we each have a big bowl of rice to mix with spicy chicken or shrimp and a fish sauce called **nuoc mam** (NOOK MOM). When I help her cook, we make **pho** (PHOH), a beef soup that has lots of noodles in it.

◀ In Vietnam, many Vietnamese buy the ingredients they need for cooking food from open-air markets.

I Am Vietnamese American

My grandmother gave me a map of Vietnam last year. I put it on the wall next to my map of the United States. She has promised me that someday we'll visit the country my family came from. My dad says that we'll also take a trip across America, to learn more about the country we live in. My mother tells us we're lucky to be able to honor the **cultures** (KUL-cherz) of two very different places. I think she's right.

Glossary

Buddhism (BOOD-izm) An Asian religion based on the teachings of the Buddha.

character (KAYR-ak-ter) A symbol used in writing or printing.

culture (KUL-cher) The beliefs, customs, and religions of a group of people.

democracy (dem-AH-kra-see) A form of government run by the people.

enlightened (en-LYT-end) Wise.

independence (in-dee-PEN-dents) Ruling oneself.

nuoc mam (NOOK MOM) Vietnamese fish sauce.

paddy (PAD-ee) Flat wetlands where rice is grown.

pho (PHOH) Vietnamese beef soup with noodles.

refugee (REF-yoo-jee) A person who leaves his or her country for a safer one.

reunite (ree-yoo-NYT) To join something back together again.

tonal (TOH-nul) Having to do with the tone or sound of something.

Index